Teach Your Dog to Talk

A Beginner's Guide to Training Your Dog to Communicate with Word Buttons

Stephanie Rocha

Published by:
Ulysses Press
PO Box 3440
Berkeley, CA 94703
www.ulyssespress.com

ISBN: 978-1-64604-254-8
Library of Congress Control Number: 2021937754

Printed in the United States by Kingery Printing Company
10 9 8 7 6 5 4 3 2 1

Acquisitions editor: Claire Sielaff
Managing editor: Claire Chun
Project editor: Renee Rutledge
Proofreader: Joyce Wu
Front cover design: Raquel Castro
Interior design and layout: what!design @ whatweb.com
Production assistant: Yesenia Garcia-Lopez

To Casper and Chico.
Thanks for being so smart and funny.

Contents

Introduction

Hello, and welcome to *Teach Your Dog to Talk*!

If you're reading these words, you obviously want to learn how to communicate with your dog or any other species of pets (cat/lizard/horse/peacock/lemur/ pig) that are currently students/learners of animal Augmentative and Alternative Communication (AAC). Even though this book is called *Teach Your Dog to Talk*, rest assured that I see you exotic animal teachers and think it's super cool that you have a "talking" iguana. Learners can be furry, scaled, or feathered, but the basics of animal AAC are essentially the same. The only difference is that you may have to modify your approach based on your learner's size or species.

Animal AAC is a relatively new phenomenon pioneered by speech-language pathologist Christina Hunger. Ms. Hunger had the bright idea of creating the first word board for her dog, Stella, a Catahoula/Australian cattle dog mix. She has also written a book called *How Stella Learned to Talk,* which is part memoir and part how-to guide. For anyone wanting to do a deep dive into the world of AAC, I recommend picking up Ms. Hunger's book, in which her experience and background shine.

Teach Your Dog to Talk focuses on some best practices being employed by learners and their teachers (pet owners) *to date.* This is to say that animal AAC is an evolving landscape. Just as with dog training, many people within the animal-training community and beyond will probably begin to develop their own opinions about and methodologies for achieving the same end goal—getting your pet to communicate effectively. Since I belong to numerous groups devoted to learning more about animal AAC, I am distilling our shared experiences into what I hope will be an informative and easy-to-follow guide for teaching your dog to talk. I am by no means an animal behavior or AAC expert, but I am an enthusiastic supporter of this movement and want to help you get started as quickly and as easily as possible.

The community of learners and teachers of animal AAC has mushroomed ever since Ms. Hunger posted an Instagram video of Stella "talking" using the Learning Resources Recordable Answer Buzzers back in October 2019. And, while those of us participating in this exciting endeavor still wonder to what extent the animals understand language, we have enough anecdotal evidence to suggest that our learners are at least communicating with us effectively.

My Talking Dog

I began teaching my dog, Casper, to use the recordable buttons in 2019, shortly after seeing Stella's videos on Instagram. Casper is a Border Aussie (50 percent border collie and 50 percent Australian shepherd). Besides his being adorable, one of the reasons I chose him was because both border collies and Australian shepherds have a fantastic working memory for language. This makes them highly trainable and, as I would come to find out, great candidates for AAC learning.

Soon after purchasing my first set of recordable buttons, I turned our dining room into a makeshift Dog Button Board Craft Workshop, much to my family's dismay. I'm pretty sure they thought I was crazy, and given that I also have a penchant for grand projects that often go unfinished, they were no doubt rolling their eyes at my latest "hobby." But there I was with some plywood, recordable buttons, and Velcro, determined to get my dog talking.

While "talking" with your dog has a very real utilitarian purpose, I have remained committed to this project because it is engaging and, oftentimes, hilarious. Casper became an accidental TikTok sensation when I posted a video of him getting mad at my daughter for not taking him on a golf cart ride. We've enjoyed all the support we've gotten online. There are still a lot of skeptics, and that's okay. Sometimes *we* don't even believe that Casper's communication skills are real.

Why I Wrote This Book

I wrote this how-to book for a couple of reasons. First, I'm the parent of an autistic child, and even though he is verbal now, years of speech therapy brought him to where he is today. His speech therapists used various forms of AAC with him, so I saw firsthand how beneficial it was and still is. That's why, when I saw Stella using her words for the first time, I thought, "Well, of *course* they can communicate!" It really resonated with me for that reason.

In *How Stella Learned to Talk*, Ms. Hunger laments the fact that more speech-language pathologists aren't trained to use AAC.[1] Hopefully, books like hers, this one, future ones, and this entire movement will bring more awareness to AAC in general. AAC tools are remarkable in that they help unlock the power of communication for those individuals who don't have the capacity for language, be they humans or animals. We're getting a window into our learners' minds, which were previously inaccessible to us because we didn't realize they could use these tools.

Giving our animal companions some power over their communication skills is really incredible. The fact is, we are seeing animals convey emotions that we wouldn't otherwise understand if they didn't have these

---

1 Christina Hunger, *How Stella Learned to Talk* (New York: HarperCollins, 2021).

devices. Casper can tell us when he's "mad" or "sad." It never gets old seeing a learner make progress and communicate something fairly complex.

I talk to Casper and our new puppy Chico's vets all the time about the animal AAC movement, which they wholeheartedly support. However, they said most vet schools don't cover much about animal emotions. One person who has interesting insight into communication is Temple Grandin, whom I learned about due to my son's autism diagnosis. She is an animal behavior expert who also happens to have autism. In a speech given to vet students at Tufts University, she said evidence is clear that animals experience fear, rage, panic, novelty seeking, and other emotions such as lust, caring, and playfulness.[2] This isn't a surprise to most pet owners, especially those of us utilizing AAC. We see our pets use words to communicate emotions on a regular basis.

It will be interesting to see what impact this movement will have on the field of veterinary medicine, animal

2   Susan Spencer, "Animal Behavior Expert Temple Grandin Tells Veterinary Students That Understanding Animals' Emotions Is Key," Telegram.com, December 2, 2015, https://www.telegram.com /article/20151201/NEWS/151209921/101371.

Teach Your Dog to Talk

behavior, and cognitive science. Given the volume of learners who are being followed by researchers at the University of California San Diego in a study run by the Comparative Cognition Lab, I can only imagine what this data will mean for them. Previously, they might have encountered one or two remarkable cases. With well over one thousand learners (and growing!) being tracked, I expect they will be able to publish some very intriguing findings.

The second reason I chose to write this is because I feel like the more information we all contribute to the collective understanding of animal AAC, the better. We are having a great time, and I think our learners are enjoying themselves as well. Because of that, I think we owe it to the movement at large to contribute as much as we can to the "hive mind" understanding of best practices and evolving technology. Most of us aren't trained professionals in cognitive science, speech pathology, or animal behavior, but as evangelists for animal AAC, we can definitely help spread the word and help others unlock the communication potential in their learners.

People ask me all the time for tips on how to get started. I've even been asked to work as a paid tutor or consultant to help people build their boards and begin working with their learner. I have no doubt an entire cottage industry will spring up around this movement. While I don't have any intention of doing this as a job, I do feel like helping people get started with this activity is a great thing to pay forward. Hopefully, this book will help in that regard.

I've always taught my dogs tricks like rolling over, crawling, or sitting up. That's something fun to do with any pet. Animal AAC is a wonderful activity that has practical implications. I'm getting to know my dogs' personalities on a much deeper level because they can now communicate their emotions to me. Many animal AAC enthusiasts have commented that their learners seem less anxious, whiny, and barky now that they can more clearly communicate their wants and needs.

What You Can Expect from This Book

You might discover that you have a very demanding animal once they learn to use their newfound skills. In addition to prepping you with a basic review of animal AAC and talking animals, this book will teach you how to navigate the tools of the trade, narrate your activities, and practice patience throughout the process.

Later in the book, we'll cover common vocabulary words to teach your pet, including why it isn't a good idea to introduce "food" or "treat" right away. This brings up a good point: don't teach your animal to use these buttons if you're not prepared to have a furry creature commanding you to attend to their every need like a tiny dictator. I love my tiny dictator, but thank goodness we have a "no" button.

Finally, we'll go over monitoring progress through what I hope will become an ongoing journey of communication and discovery. I'll provide resources and encouragement for success in the long run. Let's not forget the biggest motivation for exploring this possibility with your pet—to have fun!

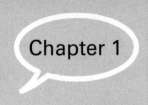

Chapter 1

Augmentative and Alternative Communication

Augmentative and Alternative Communication (AAC) is an area of clinical practice that is used by individuals who lack the capacity for verbal speech. Speech-language pathologists like Ms. Hunger work with many types of assistive devices—recordable buttons being one example—to help a nonverbal person communicate their thoughts and have their wants and needs met.

Since all animals except some birds lack the ability to speak, AAC is a great solution for them to be able to use language to communicate. Perhaps the most

Teach Your Dog to Talk

fascinating aspect of Ms. Hunger's discovery is that it wasn't made sooner. We have long known that dogs have the ability to understand language in the form of basic commands, such as "sit," "stay," "come," and "heel," and even more complex sentences. The fact that she was able to extrapolate that they might have the capacity to "talk back" is both genius and obvious. Nevertheless, kudos to her for discovering this because it's given so many of us a fun, new hobby and a window into our learners' personalities that we didn't previously have.

A Little History of "Talking" Animals

You might have heard of a border collie named Chaser who knew the name of all 1,022 of her toys. Her owner, Dr. John Pilley, was a professor of psychology who would no doubt be thrilled if he were alive to see what all these "talking" animals are doing today. While Chaser didn't actively initiate communication, her capacity for vocabulary comprehension was remarkable.

In 2018, Neil deGrasse Tyson interviewed Dr. Pilley and Chaser for an episode of *NOVA* on PBS. Dr. Tyson tested Chaser's ability to retrieve a random sampling of nine toys from a pile he had picked out from her larger, one thousand plus pile. She got all nine correct. He then added a new toy to her collection. It was a plush toy of Charles Darwin. When asked to get "Darwin"—a toy name she had never *heard* before—Chaser was able to deduce that Darwin was the toy she had never *seen* before. She took a little longer to retrieve it than the toys she already knew, but once she figured it out, she quickly retrieved it from the pile and brought it to him.[3]

Another extraordinary example of a "talking" animal was Koko the Gorilla, who was a resident of the San Francisco Zoo from 1971 until her death in 2018. She had a working vocabulary of about one thousand words as well. Koko was able to use American Sign Language to initiate communication. In using the AAC buttons, learners such as Stella are essentially doing the same thing. What's fascinating about the research being done at UCSD is that many "Chasers" and "Kokos"

---

3 NOVA PBS Official, "Chaser the Dog Shows Off Her Smarts to Neil deGrasse Tyson," August 20, 2018, https://youtu.be/omaHv5sxiFl.

are being observed, so this study is unusual in size and scope.

On the flip side of this phenomenon, it's worth mentioning something called the "Clever Hans effect." Clever Hans was a German horse that was famous for being able to perform arithmetic and other tasks in the early 1900s. However, a psychologist named Oskar Pfungst investigated and realized that the horse wasn't actually doing any of the tasks, but rather watching his trainer for a reaction. In other words, Clever Hans was responding to the involuntary cues and body language of his trainer who was, of course, unaware that he was providing any of these cues.

Because there is still much research to be done on animal AAC, it's unclear how much a teacher's subconscious cues could be influencing the communication of their learner. Studying all of these new AAC learners will be the life's work of many animal behaviorists, cognitive scientists, and others in related fields. It's worth being intentionally neutral as your learner begins to use the buttons to avoid any possibility of triggering the Clever Hans effect.

Talking Animal Pioneers

To say that the talking animal movement has taken off is an understatement! Do a search of any of the following hashtags on either Instagram or TikTok and you will find tons of enjoyable content related to the animal AAC world:

#TheyCanTalk

#TalkingDog

#FluentPet

#ButtonTraining

#MyDogTalks

#Hunger4Words (named after Ms. Hunger's blog)

As a community, there has been some concern that using the #AAC hashtag for animals might prevent people searching for AAC resources for humans from finding relevant content. But #AnimalAAC, #DogAAC, #CanineAAC, #CatAAC, or #FelineAAC would probably work. Hashtags are a moving target, so keep exploring to see what pulls up the most relevant content for you. YouTube also has a lot of tutorials, so definitely subscribe to channels that seem most applicable to your learner and situation.

When you are first starting out, it is super helpful to find some learners who are similar to yours, whether they're the same species or breed. They can be virtual mentors—just like Stella and Ms. Hunger were for us.

Getting Started

Please note that teaching your animal to communicate using AAC isn't for everyone. We've all done just fine having animal companions who understand simple verbal commands and communicate back to us in a nonverbal way. My family's dog growing up had different pitches of barking to let us know what he needed. He also understood basic obedience commands. I'd venture to say we understood each other 99.9 percent of the time. So, if you try this and for whatever reason it doesn't work out, don't despair. Our pets will still find a way to let us know what's up.

Embarking on this journey requires a commitment to the process in addition to the end goal. Some dogs and animals will pick this up very quickly while others may be scared, try to play with or destroy the buttons, or simply show zero interest at first. Some learners have caught on in six days and others have taken six months. There isn't really a way to know how long it will take for your learner to grasp the concept.

Before we knew about the buttons, we had trained Casper to use a call bell near his bowl to signal that he was hungry, and potty bells that hung on the front door for him to signal us he needed to go outside. That made transitioning to buttons easier because he was already using these two different bells as AAC devices. However, it initially took some time for him to learn to use the bells when we first introduced them. With that in mind, consider that some learners might take a while to master their first button. That's why above all else, the key to teaching your dog to talk is *patience*. To use a popular saying, "It's a marathon, not a sprint." Even if your goal is to teach your learner a limited number of words (ten or fewer), you'll want to go slowly and follow some guidelines that seem to work for a large number of successful talking animals (see Chapters 3 and 4 for the guidelines I've provided in this book).

As you read this guide, also allow yourself to get creative with your learner. Just because something worked for *one* dog (or cat or horse), doesn't mean it will work for your learner. Sure, we are all following some basic guidelines, but every learner is different, so meet them where they are and find that path of least resistance. By that I mean, be willing to change things on the fly if they don't seem to be working. Even though I'm writing this guide and will try to cover as much ground as possible, there is no way to go into detail for every scenario you might encounter. That's why the collaborative online groups are so helpful. Make sure you join some of them, which I will cover in the Resources chapter (page 118) so you can share any cool tips and tricks with other AAC enthusiasts. We're all learning as we go, and our collective knowledge is so valuable to this movement.

There's even a research group that is a collaboration between CleverPet (maker of the FluentPet products that I'll cover on page 27) and the University of California San Diego. You can enroll by going to this link: https://survey.zohopublic.com/zs/t4BU6s

Now, let's get talking!

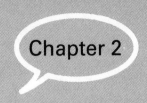

Chapter 2

Tools and Devices

"Can we build it?"

"YES! WE! CAN!"

My kids grew up watching *Bob the Builder,* so I hear this phrase from the cartoon in my head anytime I think about starting a new project. That was certainly the case when I saw Stella's word board for the first time. I remember staring at her videos in awe, thinking to myself, "What? Dogs can communicate with words?"

Following this revelation, I couldn't fill up my Amazon shopping cart fast enough.

Label maker: "Add to cart!"

MDF board: "Add to cart!"

Velcro: "Add to cart!"

Batteries: "Add to cart!" (Rechargeable batteries are probably better for the planet and your wallet, even though they are a little more expensive up front.)

And, finally...the Learning Resources Recordable Answer Buzzers: "ADD. TO. CART!" (These are the recordable buttons that Ms. Hunger used to build Stella's word board and still uses today.)

So confident that my dog would be learning this new skill, I initially bought two sets of the Learning Resources buttons for a total of eight buttons. I suggest starting with just one set unless you, too, possess an overinflated confidence in your abilities to be an AAC guru right out of the gate. The Learning Resources buttons were designed for humans, but they do work well for most dogs and cats.

There is as much of a learning curve for you (the teacher) as there is for your learner. Modeling the buttons as you see many of us doing in our videos is a lot of work. Even if you have children (and obviously taught them to talk), this is unlike anything you would have done with them, assuming they didn't need AAC. Modeling the button usage is one of the most important aspects of animal AAC when you first get started because you are helping your learner make the association between the buttons and the action or thing it represents.

Building Your First Word Board

As of this writing, there are two main options for recordable buttons that you can use on your word board, although I've seen some variations people have purchased in other countries.

The original talking dog, Stella, began with and still uses the Learning Resources Recordable Answer Buzzers, and it appears Ms. Hunger is now selling her own branded version of these on her website, hungerforwords.com. These include a guide, so they are more expensive at $27.99 for four buttons. Normally they range between $15 and $20 per set. These buttons were not made for animals, but can be modified to be more animal friendly. For instance, some people have put nonslip coverings on top to keep paws and claws from slipping off the button as easily.

The other buttons on the market that we currently use are manufactured by FluentPet. They are smaller, animal friendly, and fit nicely into proprietary HexTiles that they also manufacture. The hexagonal-shaped tiles are made out of foam and have slots that fit either the FluentPet or the Learning Resources buttons in them.

As I mentioned, a few other recordable buttons are available, depending on where you live. I suspect that other companies will also get into the animal AAC game. Given that our community of 1,500 participants is growing every day, it's possible that AAC will entail its own cottage industry within the overall pet industry, which reached $99 billion in the United States in 2020.[4]

The HexTiles look similar to this:

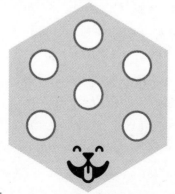

---

4 Sanela Puac, "22 Fascinating Pet Industry Statistics & Facts for 2021," May 18, 2021, https://petpedia.co/pet-industry-statistics/.

Instead of buying premade HexTiles, you can build your own board made of wood, cork, or floor foam.

- ❖ Wood. The buttons can be mounted on a simple piece of plywood or MDF that you can purchase at a home improvement store or Amazon. If you go this route, you will need something to attach them to the board, which is where the Velcro comes in. Just make sure that you don't cover over the battery compartment because you will need access to change out the batteries from time to time if you are using the buttons from Learning Resources.

- ❖ Cork. Similar to the wood, but since it is softer, you can make a cutout for the button, which would mean you wouldn't need the Velcro. Or, you can just mount them in a similar way. The advantage of the cork is that it's lightweight and inexpensive.

- ❖ Floor foam. The HexTiles from FluentPet are made out of foam, but you can just buy any interlocking floor foam, and cut the holes for the buttons. Again, this is a lightweight and inexpensive option.

Whether you intend to use premade HexTiles or a simple piece of wood, cork, or floor foam, you will want to preplan your board by word groupings or categories.

We'll go into vocabulary planning later in this guide, but the quick-start advice here is to begin with two words, such as "outside" and "play." Avoid using "treat" or "food" since most learners tend to overuse those buttons when they first get them, and you can't possibly reinforce their request by feeding them every time they ask for a treat or food. However, it's possible you could quickly play with them or step outside to help them correlate the button press with the action.

Labeling

It is very important to label the buttons clearly so you can press the relevant one quickly in order to reinforce to your learner where it is located on the board. I don't own a Cricut machine (although I seriously considered buying one for this). For the uninitiated, a Cricut machine can create any number of custom-cut designs on paper, leather, and vinyl. Several Etsy sellers have created some awesome templates you can download for creating button labels with your Cricut.

The buttons need to have large icons or words on them so you can see them when standing above the board. The labeling is for you, not your learner. Although maybe animals learning to read is the next step. Please keep us posted if your dog requests a subscription to the *New York Times*.

Floor or Wall?

It's important to establish up front whether you think your learner will use their snout or paw. If you think they might be more inclined to use their nose, word boards can be mounted on the wall for a learner to more easily use their snout. The majority of learners use their paws or a combination of paw and snout; for them, the word boards work just fine on the floor.

One pro of a wall-mounted word board is that they are more space friendly, so if you don't have a lot of room, I would explore this as an option. Another benefit is they're also much cleaner because dirt and hair won't accumulate on the tiles or around the buttons. The con of a wall-mounted board is that, once your learner catches on, they need to turn around to look at you for a reaction. (See page 40 for more on this.)

Number of Words

Most learners start out with four to eight buttons. The reason is that the Learning Resources buttons come in sets of four.

As a teacher, eight buttons may be all you ever want or need. Decide roughly how many words you ultimately want to teach your learner before you build your board and leave room for expansion if possible. I will warn you that this is an addictive activity, and it's really easy to get carried away. In our growing community of teachers, some people are happy if their learner can just communicate the basics ("food," "water," "play," and "outside," for example), while others are letting their learner's progress dictate how many words they add.

In any case, it's helpful to have a target number of words so you can space the buttons out, giving your learner room to navigate the board without accidentally pressing other buttons. I definitely made the mistake of putting Casper's first set of buttons too close together, and he often pressed buttons by accident because there wasn't enough space between each one.

Word count is also a consideration when it comes to space in your home. Until we moved just recently, Casper's word board took up a substantial amount of space in our kitchen.

Buttons

Whether you go with the Learning Resources buttons or begin with the FluentPet version, you'll find they operate in a similar way. To use one, you'll press a small record button located on the side to record yourself saying the word you've chosen. You'll hear a beep, say the word, and then press the top of the button to hear the word. You may need to speak a little louder and overenunciate your word to make sure it's clear in the recording.

The difference with the FluentPet product is that you can lock the record button so your learner doesn't accidentally record over your word if they hit it with their paw. If you use the FluentPet HexTiles with the Learning Resources buttons, it helps a little because they sit inside a cutout space for the button. However, it's still possible for your learner to reset the Learning Resources button. If that happens a lot, either space out the buttons to give your learner more room or switch to the FluentPet buttons.

It's also worth mentioning that the size and structure of the buttons may make one a better choice over the other, but that will largely depend on your learner's species, breed, and size. It ultimately boils down to your personal preference and how efficiently your learner can use the buttons. Some teachers have found that the FluentPet buttons are too small and harder for their large-breed dogs to accurately press due to their paw size. On the flip side, the Learning Resources buttons are not as durable and tend to break easily, and their sound quality degrades over time.

In the end, the right button choice is the one that fits your budget and learner's style. The same goes for the setup and whether you use a DIY board or a HexTile. Most of us start off with the Learning Resources buttons and still use them in some capacity. For instance, I'm using the Learning Resources button for my puppy, Chico. He's in that gangly teenager phase and doesn't have great control of his paws, so the larger buttons are easier for him to use.

Start off slowly so you can make sure that the buttons you choose will work long term.

Learning Resources vs. FluentPet

The Learning Resources buttons are slightly more accessible—especially internationally—than the FluentPet buttons as of this writing. They are also less expensive, which is definitely a consideration when you are starting out. One single FluentPet button is $12.95; or, you can buy eighteen for $129.95, which brings the cost down to $7.22 per button. In contrast, the Learning Resources buttons are $19.95 for four (about $5.00 each).

Your pet may or may not show interest in this activity, so start conservatively with a small board and one set of Learning Resources buttons (four). Then you can decide whether to continue building out your word board with those or transition to the FluentPet buttons, which are built specifically for animal AAC.

If you decide to switch from one brand to the other, it is important to do this in such a way that your learner doesn't get confused. Speaking from personal experience, we totally confused Casper. Luckily, there are many resources online for transitioning from one to the other, so definitely review those posts or videos.

We had built a fairly substantial word board with the Learning Resources buttons, but it was also taking up a lot of floor space. The FluentPet buttons appealed to us since they are smaller. Also, the sound quality is much better.

Once our new buttons arrived, I rerecorded his vocabulary onto the new setup and, uh, well... that didn't work. Casper ignored the new buttons for almost a week. Even though this wasn't the "right" way to transition, it was interesting to see how he taught himself where the new buttons were on the word board. He would casually just walk across the board hitting random buttons that made no sense whatsoever. After about seven to eight days of this, one day he hit "Mama, Love You!" and then turned around and looked at me. Of course I melted, and to make sure I reinforced this interaction, I went over to his board and hit, "Casper, Mama, Love You!"

In reviewing several people's experiences with transitioning to a new word board, it seems that following your learner's lead is key. If you feel like you could move several words at a time without skipping a beat, go for it. Most learners will require a transition period, however. Placing your original word board near the one you are transitioning to will help this go more smoothly. Move one or two buttons per day and model the new buttons to help your learner acclimate.

There have been teachers who start with the FluentPet buttons and go back to the Learning Resources buttons, so the same concept would apply. It's worth mentioning that some people also decide to scale back their word board if their learner isn't using some of the words on it. If your learner is only using four to six buttons consistently and that is working for them, there's no need for a bigger word board.

Observe Your Own Words

Observe which words you use in your household before deciding on what to use on your board. Also pay attention to how your learner reacts to those words. Casper responded with nonverbal cues such as barking, tilting his head, whining, and wagging his tail. This let us know that he understood what we were saying. You want to use high-value words, or words that get your learner's attention.

Many of us have set up our learners' word boards using the HexTiles, which follow a modified version of the Fitzgerald Key. The Fitzgerald Key was created in the early 1900s by Edith Fitzgerald, a deaf American teacher. Her system organized vocabulary into categories, which enabled hearing-impaired students to use grammar and syntax. When the founders of FluentPet designed their hexagonal tiles, they loosely based them on this concept to potentially help the animal learners do the same thing. Words are grouped into who, what, where, doing, descriptors, and social words (see the illustration on page 39).

However, the actual words you use can vary greatly. One learner may use "food" while another says "hungry" or "eat" to communicate their desire for a meal. This is totally fine, but your learner's words need to closely mirror how you would speak to your dog or other people in your house about a certain activity or feeling.

Since we have used both a rectangular, homemade board and the HexTiles, I can say that both work equally well. However, having the words grouped logically, particularly with a hexagonal setup, is a huge help to me; I imagine that they also help the learner compartmentalize where words are situated on the board. If you plan on growing your learner's vocabulary, the HexTiles are great because they are so naturally expandable.

Below is a blank template you can use to sketch out which words you might want to use and, ultimately, how big you want your word board to be. I've also included an example of a simple rectangular grid.

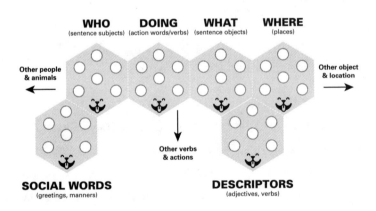

SAMPLE WORD BOARD

WHO
- MOM
- DAD
- FRIEND
- LEARNER NAME

DOING
- PLAY
- HELP
- COME
- GO

WHERE
- BED
- OUTSIDE
- KENNEL
- WALK

SOCIAL WORDS
- LOVE YOU
- WHERE
- YES
- WANT

DESCRIPTORS
- ALL DONE
- GOOD
- MAD
- LATER

WHAT
- CAR
- FOOD
- WATER
- TOY

Space and Access

Whether you decide to let your word board grow organically as your learner progresses or you decide that you will only have a total of X number of words, make sure that the buttons are properly spaced so your learner can easily step between them as they begin to use multiple buttons.

If you are starting out with the buttons being close to the thing they are referencing (for example, "outside" or "potty" being close to the door), consider where you might set up your board once you consolidate the buttons. Or, you may never consolidate the buttons and simply keep them contextually located. A "hungry" or "food" button could be strategically placed near your learner's bowls. Wherever you choose to locate them, the key is setting them up where you spend time and can model using them for your learner.

It would be ideal if the word board is situated in an area where your learner can access the buttons from more than one side. This will prevent them from having to crane their neck back around or go to too much effort to check for your reaction. This look for our reaction is one of the ways many of us report knowing that our dogs or animals are using the buttons intentionally. It's worth watching some of the videos under the #FluentPet or #TheyCanTalk hashtag to get a feel for how common this is. In addition to placing the board where your learner can easily access it, the board should be in an area where you hang out most of the time, such as a kitchen or living room area.

The idea of having a giant word board sitting on your living room or kitchen floor might deter you from this endeavor. I love watching Bunny (@whataboutbunny on Instagram) or Bastian (@bastianandbrews) using their sizable word boards to communicate very complex thoughts. However, the notion that everyone has that amount of real estate in their home to devote to their dog may be unrealistic. For most owners, four to eight words is all that's needed to give their learner the tools to communicate basic needs.

As I mentioned, many teachers report that their learners whine and bark less once they learn to use animal AAC. I know that is certainly the case with Casper, who, before learning to use the buttons, would whine incessantly, hoping we would magically understand exactly what he wanted. Eight words should give you enough vocabulary to cover "outside," "walk," "food," "water," "potty," "play," "scritches," and "treat," for example. Adding in additional vocabulary for more abstract concepts and verbs is certainly rewarding because you start to get more insight into their thinking process. However, don't feel pressured to let the buttons take over your kitchen. If you do choose to expand your learner's vocabulary, just plan accordingly. Because this is such a fun activity, it's easy to see why some teachers are giving up their living room space to accommodate their learners' giant word boards.

Lights! Camera! Action!

Depending on how fast (or slow) you are with your smartphone, you might want to invest in a motion-activated camera to record your learner's interactions with their word board. This will help to both chart your progress later on and interpret what your learner might be trying to say. Unless you are near the word board all the time, you could miss a valuable interaction.

For instance, some teachers have reported that if their learner is missing a word for a specific thing, their dog has used a combination of words to express what they want. One example I recall was a dog who liked to chew on ice. They did not have the word for ice on their word board at the time but did have the words "water" and "bone," which they pressed simultaneously on more than one occasion. What this particular teacher realized was that a "water bone" was their learner trying to say "ice." Once she added the word "ice" to the word board, the dog began using that word instead. A camera that is recording all the time would enable you to pick up on word combinations such as this to help you determine what word(s) to add next.

Some possible options for motion-activated recording are:

- ☸ Wyze video camera–$30 to $35 (They make a pet version that can move around.)
- ☸ Furbo—$170 (This also dispenses treats.)
- ☸ Various cameras on Amazon (read the reviews first!)–$30 to $70
- ☸ Old smartphone using an app called Alfred, which turns it into a pet cam

Choose video-editing software according to personal preference and technical capability. Both app stores for iOS and Android should have a good selection. I love Quik, Premiere Rush, and Pro Camera by Moment. For generating subtitles automatically, which most of us use to display the videos online, Clipomatic is wonderful.

Posting videos to social media is a great way to introduce your learner to the community and get to know other teachers. If you choose to be part of the TheyCanTalk.org community, this video evidence will contribute to their growing body of research on this phenomenon.

Tracking Progress

We'll get into this in more detail in Chapter 5 but, assuming you have invested this much effort into teaching your animal to communicate, you might want to keep track of their progress. I'm old school and just use a simple notebook, but some very smart people in our community have developed various sophisticated methods for tracking their learner's progress.

One teacher even built her dog Honey Butter (@Honey ButterTalks on Instagram) a computer, or "dogputer," if you will, during quarantine using some items from the hardware store and Raspberry Pi (a tiny, programmable computer). Honestly, this just puts all of our craftiness to shame. Her button presses are auto*magic*ally fed into a Google spreadsheet, and her owner uses Google Studio to visualize the data. It's all very high tech and very cool. If you're not familiar with Google Studio, it's a free tool that turns your data into informative, easy-to-read, easy-to-share, and fully customizable dashboards and reports. Definitely worth checking out if you love seeing your data visually represented.

Another teacher who has two learners (dogs named Dewey and Dusty) (@Dewey_Doodling on Instagram) has created a similar dashboard using Google Studio. It tracks daily words, word use/frequency, and use by time of day, and shows fourteen-day progress. Again, you can track all of these things manually using a daily planner, but I'm in awe of the creativity and resourcefulness that exists within the animal AAC community.

If you do choose to go the low-tech route, create a worksheet that looks something like the daily progress sheet to follow. Print and bind a stack of worksheets at your local office supply store to create a little progress journal.

(Name of Learner)'s AAC Daily Progress Sheet

Date started:

Today's date:

Week #:

New words:

Word	Number of times used

Time of day most active (this is where the video camera footage will help):

Notes:

Whatever method you use is correct. There is no right or wrong way to do this (you don't even have to keep track of their progress), but it is useful to do something, even if it's very basic. One teacher I spoke to said she uses a whiteboard and then snaps a photo at the end of each day and saves it to a folder on her phone. She can then quickly flip through the photos by date to see how her learner—a dog—is progressing.

When we first started, we were very consistent with tracking Casper's progress. Now that he's reached what will probably be the maximum number of words he uses (thirty-six), we aren't as diligent about it. However, I've started the entire process over with Chico, so I will definitely be back in tracking-progress mode.

Travel and Portability

While FluentPet *does* make an accessory for traveling with your buttons called a Soundboard Carrier, it might be worth having a more compact, separate set just for traveling. We've never been in another place away from home long enough to justify lugging Casper's entire word board with us. We take three or four buttons just to cover the basics. However, I think that if it's possible to bring your word board with you, it would help your learner cope with new environments and situations. It would also reinforce the language concepts that they are learning because "outside" will refer to a different place but the same concept.

I haven't seen a travel setup for the Learning Resources buttons, so you will need to bring your tiny screwdriver and take the batteries out *before* you hit the road.

Otherwise, you'll get serenaded by a chorus of button recordings every time you hit a bump in the road. Been there, done that.

I'm sure many of us are hoping that as the tools and technology evolve, we will someday have a type of mat that can easily be rolled up and tucked into a suitcase. I would imagine we are just on the cusp of some really interesting new devices that our learners can use both at home and on the road. Of course, the ultimate dream would be the collar that translates our dog's thoughts into words like the one Dug had in the movie *Up*. And, I'm quite sure Casper would say, "My mom is good and smart."

Remember that AAC doesn't have to be only using buttons. When we are on the go, we sometimes use alternate forms of AAC, just as we used the bells before we even knew about word buttons.

We have trained Casper to answer yes/no questions using our right hand for yes and left for no. We can usually figure out what he needs by asking a series of questions and noting his responses.

To make sure his answers are *mostly* accurate, we will ask him a few questions we know he would say "no" to before we begin, such as "Would you like to take a bath?" If he says "yes," then we know he's not engaged because he never *wants* to take a bath. But, assuming he answers those test questions accurately, we can figure out what he needs by process of elimination.

As I said, if you do take your word board on the road, you might want to pare it down to the absolute fewest words your learner would need to get their needs met. Several teachers have reported that their learners are less anxious in new places when they can access their word boards to communicate.

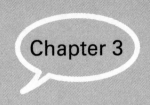

Chapter 3

Prepping for Success

As with any type of animal training, the main key is consistency. Dogs learn through mimicry, so modeling using the word board and rewarding your learner for mirroring your behavior is also important.

Training the Trainer (or Teacher)

Trainers will tell you that training the pet owner is as critical as training the pet. Since animal AAC is an evolving field of study, not many offer an in-person service, so you become an effective teacher by training yourself using resources such as this book and other online resources. The TheyCanTalk.org community created by the founders of FluentPet is an expanding wiki of community experiences and feedback, and a few trainers participate and help other teachers in their journey. The trainers I spoke to agree that some of the same rules for teaching basic obedience and other positive behaviors apply to teaching animal AAC, such as:

- 🐾 Avoid accidental feedback for negative behavior. Put another way, ignore unwanted behavior and show approval for positive interactions with the word board.

- 🐾 Provide structure. In this context, the word board is used for a specific purpose: to communicate with you. It is not a toy nor is it to be abused just for the purpose of getting treats.

- 🐾 Make it portable. Being able to transport at least some portion of the word board to other settings, such as when you travel or your learner stays with a dog sitter or family member, will be key in helping reinforce how they use the word board, regardless of where they are.

Behavior Modifications...for the Teacher

Trainers and teachers agree that teaching your pet to talk may require some behavior modification on your part. Here are some tips on where to start:

- 🐾 Talk to your pet more than you currently do. Exposing your learner to new words and concepts verbally will help them connect the dots when you introduce the buttons.

- 🐾 Use high-value words. These are words you know your learner understands and can use to get their attention. There's a cute popular trend online where you talk to your dog using their favorite words and watch their facial expressions change with each mention of that word. Take note of which words get your learner's attention, as these may be some of the best words to start with. "Golf cart" was Casper's high-value phrase, so of course we added that right away. We did a video where we told Casper that we went to the *dog park* in the *golf cart* and ate *bacon*. I'm sure he was totally confused, but the key was that those are all high-value words to him and he definitely perked up when he heard them. Our animals definitely understand quite a lot!

🐾 Narrate your day. Just like children, dogs learn by listening before they can "talk" themselves. Your conversations will seem one-sided, but we know that animals absorb language or else they wouldn't be able to follow basic obedience commands. Rest assured they are observing and absorbing what you are saying. It just may take a while before they can use what they are hearing to communicate back to you.

🐾 Ask your dog questions. While your learner won't be able to respond, simply hearing the inflection in your voice that normally happens when you ask a question will prime them for potentially being able to respond once they learn how to use the buttons.

🐾 Repetition is important. As they hear you use your native language vocabulary to speak to them over and over, they will eventually catch on and be able to use those words to communicate back to you.

Keep sentence structure simple. Don't use pronouns when talking to your learner. Bunny (@whataboutbunny) appears to be grasping the concept of pronouns, but I think this would be rare for most learners. Casper uses his own name to refer to himself, and we don't plan on changing that.

Model, Model, Model!

Now that you are talking to your dog and have chosen the right words, it's time to model using the buttons. What does this mean? Modeling is a sequence of saying the word, pressing the button, and then performing the action. It helps your learner associate the button with the word, and the word with the action.

Start with one-word phrases in the form of a question, such as "Walk?" When you ask your dog if they want to go for a walk, you would say the phrase out loud then press the button that says "walk." Repeat this several times for practice. After that, grab the leash and go outside for a short walk. Eventually, your learner should catch on that they can *request* a walk by doing the same thing.

Continue to narrate activities using simplified sentence structure so that when you decide to add words, your dog may already be familiar enough with the phrase that they will catch on more quickly. You can then move on to two- and three-word phrases that might include the learner's name, such as "Casper," "Go," "Walk."

Depending on how many buttons you begin with, your dog will most likely memorize the placement of the buttons on your word board, but you will need to label them for your own purposes. As I mentioned, we have tons of crafty people in our community who make vinyl stickers with icons for their word buttons. You can use a label maker or paint pen, too. Whatever makes it easy for you to quickly identify a button so you can model a phrase immediately.

As I noted in Chapter 2, you have to spend time teaching your dog to press the buttons. The recordable buttons from Learning Resources weren't made for animals, but they work fine. If you're willing to make some modifications for button texture or sound quality, they are even better. I also previously mentioned that FluentPet manufactures custom-made buttons designed specifically for animal AAC. Regardless of which buttons you choose, modeling using the buttons is how your learner will catch on to what they do.

If you've used a clicker or treats to train your dog to do other tricks, you can do the same thing by rewarding your dog for interacting with the buttons. Smaller dogs or animals might have some difficulty at first with getting the buttons to activate using their paw. Several teachers have been successful teaching their learners to press the buttons with their snout and even mounted the buttons on the wall to make that action easier. Depending on your dog's size, you'll have to experiment with what works best.

"Use Your Words"

This is something parents say to our children when they first acquire language. Whenever they point or make nonverbal noises to communicate, we tell them to "use their words." Likewise, you can encourage your learner to use their words and even gesture toward their word board. However, it's never a good idea to tell your learner to say a specific word, because you want them to initiate communication and choose the right word for the situation.

If you notice your learner trying to communicate with you nonverbally, it's okay to encourage them to use their word board either by standing next to it, modeling a button press of what you think they are trying to say, or simply pointing at the board. The goal is to retrain them to use language instead of nonverbal cues such as whining or barking.

Once you tell them to "use their words," give them the space and time to do so. Language processing time in animals can be very slow, and it's easy to get impatient. Try to be patient and let them get out what they need to say. Always provide praise and positive feedback when they get it right! You can even respond to accidental presses by doing whatever your learner accidentally hit. The point is, using the buttons or "using their words" is a big accomplishment, and you want to encourage them to keep it up.

Target Practice

Pressing buttons is not a normal animal activity or behavior. Before you start, you may even need to get your learner to the point of understanding *how* the buttons work. Some learners seem to pick up this unnatural behavior right away while others will need coaxing and positive reinforcement. For example, you may need to place their paw or nose on the button until it makes a sound and then reward them with a treat. Some teachers feel like this isn't a good idea and only the "treat" button should result in the learner getting an actual treat. While this does make sense, the goal is to get your learner using the buttons, so I think that decision can be left up to the individual teacher.

Once they get the hang of button pressing, then you can move on to doing the action indicated by that button. Dog behaviorist and trainer Kate Naito offers a great YouTube video on using sticky notes to progressively work up to using a button (or bell) to get your dog to communicate (see "Teach Your Dog to Push a Button [or Ring a Bell] to Go Outside," by BKLN Manners: Urban Dog Training). You'll want to make sure your learner is proficient at this action before you move beyond the first button. Also, it's probably a good idea to leave the button sound off (it will make a clicking sound when the dog has successfully pushed it) or record a neutral sound like a whistle or squeaky toy that doesn't mean anything while they are learning. If you are offering a treat for your learner to press the button and it says "play," then they might begin to think that "play" is synonymous with "treat."

For smaller animals, the FluentPet buttons don't require as much pressure to activate, so consider those over the Learning Resources buttons if you have a small dog, cat, or other animal that might have difficulty activating the buttons.

Exploration Phase

Depending on how many words you introduce at one time, your dog may take an interest in exploring the buttons. This might include sniffing them, pawing at them, attempting to play with them, or unintentionally pressing them to see what they do. If your learner tries to destroy them, obviously remove them from view. However, as long as your learners are showing some sort of interest in the word board or individual buttons, you should continue to encourage them. Show some excitement or even give them a few scritches behind their ears to cement a positive connection between your learner and the word board.

Whenever we rearrange or move Casper's buttons, he explores by pressing all the buttons nonsensically, perhaps to reorient himself with the location of the words. Who knows? The point is, any interaction that isn't destructive should be encouraged. Using hand gestures or going over to the board to press a button is also helpful as they learn how all of this language stuff works.

In this phase, you can choose to respond to random button presses to help your learner make the connection. If your learner accidentally presses "play," for instance, take a minute to play with them. Sometimes it's not possible to do the thing the button says, but if it is, take that opportunity to help them connect the word button to an action. You can model it by pressing it again intentionally and then performing the action.

Teach Your Dog to Talk

Reinforcing the Connection

The day your learner presses a button and then looks at you for a reaction is when you know that they are trying to communicate with you. Intentional presses are magical because you can almost see the dog thinking. There can be a long pause between words that make up a phrase—sometimes up to thirty seconds because dogs seem to process language more slowly. Even if your learner just presses one button carefully and then looks to you for a reaction, it is important to honor the request or command to reinforce that the buttons help your learner get what they need and want. For example, if your learner presses "outside," then you need to take them outside right away to connect the dots between the button and the action.

As I said, when first starting out, your learner may seem confused and press the buttons in a nonsensical way. That's okay, and that's what Casper did. Other teachers have reported this same type of interaction with the word boards, so it seems logical to say this is a common behavior.

The only time we discourage using the buttons is when Casper is overstimulated or impatient because we aren't understanding what he wants. He wildly presses multiple buttons that make no sense. In these instances, we don't—nor could we—respond to every button press, so we simply redirect him to another activity until he can use the board properly.

Practice Patience

Patience is *so* important with your new learner. As noted, this is not a natural interaction for them, so consistency and patience are really the keys to success, from what we've seen with other animals. It might take four to six weeks before you see a button press that is contextually appropriate. After that initial connection, hopefully you will be able to add more buttons at a time and at a faster clip. However, it's important that you make sure your learner is truly using those first one or two buttons correctly before investing any more time or money into buying more buttons.

Patience is also important when you see your learner taking an interest in the buttons. Resist the temptation to overstimulate them and instead remain quiet. If your learner is exploring or even has used a button, wait for them to look to at you for a reaction. We'll talk more about how important simply waiting (not reacting) to respond to your learner is once you get into three- and four-word phrases.

Another critical component of being patient is learning to read nonverbal cues. As I mentioned in the first chapter, I had a dog who had different pitches of barking and whining. We could tell the difference between a "hungry" whine and a "potty" whine. We knew a "bored" bark from a "danger" bark. Looking back, I see how attuned we all were to these nonverbal cues. Similarly, being patient with your learner to figure out what they are trying to communicate can help you predict which button might work for that situation. If you have a good nonverbal communicator, you can begin to transition your learner to using the buttons, which will hopefully cut down on the barking or whining.

Age of the Learner

We recently adopted a puppy, who is Casper's half-brother from the same dad. Hopefully, he will have the same aptitude for language that Casper has. I get a lot of direct messages on Instagram related to when someone should begin teaching their learner. I'm sure someone with training in animal cognition might have a better answer to this question, but anecdotally, what I'm seeing is that as soon as your dog can understand some basic obedience commands—which is language—then they can potentially begin to make the connection between the words and the buttons. That doesn't mean they will begin using them any time soon, but if you are consistently modeling the button usage along with the words, they should eventually catch on and make the connection. I would think a lot depends on what species your learner is, and then, of course, what breed.

There are many examples of teachers working with learners as young as eight to ten weeks old. However, there are also dogs in the double digits who have figured out how to use AAC. Some of them started with the potty bells and then transitioned to the buttons/

word board. It really depends on your learner and how diligent you are with their training. Most animal training requires a certain level of consistency. This is especially so with AAC training because it is so novel. We've only scratched the surface in terms of what this will mean for animals long term.

Regression

Casper kind of regressed a couple of times. Not only did he stop using his words when we transitioned him to a new board (and then again when we moved to a new house), but he cut down on the number of words he used consistently. Whereas he was using multiple words in an almost sentence-like way—"Casper" "want" "food"—he simply began pressing "food" when he was hungry. In fact, he really stopped using his name altogether and was much less interested in the complexity of the interaction. In doing the research for this book, I found that this was not unusual and happened for various reasons.

One learner I read about in our group had been doing great, but then began mixing up the meaning of certain words. For example, he was pressing "outside" when he clearly wanted "dinner." Of course, this can be super frustrating, especially if you've been at it for a while and your learner was seemingly doing really well. In our case, we simply scaled back Casper's board for a few weeks and only kept the bare necessities out, which we modeled like crazy. Even if we were all the way across the room getting ready to head outside, we ran over to the board to press "outside." We gradually added back the rest of his core words and then the more complex words until all thirty-six words were back on the grids.

Limit Distractions

As with any training, getting your learner to focus on using the buttons means limiting outside influences, which could distract them. Keeping the noise level, such as that from the TV or music, turned down or off and avoiding trying to teach them during a busy time of day will ensure they absorb more of what you show them. This will also help you, the teacher, to stay focused and keep track of their progress.

Make sure your learner isn't hungry, sleepy, or thirsty, and that they don't need to go outside, as these could all be distractions as well. Meet your learner's basic needs and keep training sessions short. This will help them stay focused and retain more of what you are modeling.

Everyone On Board

I'm in the middle of obedience training with our puppy, Chico, who is only three months old. I'd forgotten just how important it is for ALL of us—even though I'm the primary trainer—to be on the same page with regard to his training. Teaching him something as basic as not pulling on his leash when we go for a walk requires consistent redirection. If I'm the only one who does that even though there are three of us who walk him, he will keep up the negative behavior. The same goes with using AAC. Consistency is the key to success.

If all members of the household aren't willing to use AAC in a way that's similar to how you (the primary teacher) do, it's better if they don't use it at all. It will just confuse your learner and potentially set them up to have a negative association with their word board if they are getting confused. Modeling is the most important thing to be consistent about. As I mentioned earlier, it's a lot of work and not a natural thing we would normally do when teaching a neurotypical human to talk. Teaching your animal learner what the button means and showing them where it is on the word board requires you to use it a lot—especially in the beginning. Encourage everyone to do this if possible.

One teacher whose video I watched uses a menu board that is propped up in her kitchen, where other members of the family can see it. She has a space for the Word of the Week, where she puts the new word that was introduced that week. She also has a Top 3 Words area, where she lists the words her learner used the most. She said this keeps everyone engaged with their new rescue dog, whom she began training as soon as she got him. The point is, whatever you are doing, try to get the whole household involved and on the same page, if possible.

If At First You Don't Succeed...

I'm sure this book will go to print and I'll have a <facepalm> moment when I'll wonder why I forgot to include something important in this chapter. The overarching advice here is that persistence and patience will usually pay off, but don't feel bad if your learner takes a lot longer than others or simply never catches on. While it *is* a fun activity, it can have its ups and downs.

Before I got interested in AAC with Casper, I was going to look into dock diving as a sport for him. There was only one problem: he's terrified of the water. Your learner may never get used to the idea of pressing buttons to communicate with you, but there are so many other activities you can do with your animal companion, so don't give up searching for another activity in case this doesn't work.

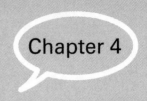

Chapter 4

All about Words

Because this is all still new territory for so many of us, we are learning from not only Ms. Hunger's work, but from each other as well. Word choice, when/how to introduce new words, and interpreting what our learners are trying to communicate can get a little overwhelming. Once again, start slowly and be patient. Beyond that, be willing to change things up if they aren't working.

First Words

One of the questions all animal AAC teachers get asked most frequently is which word to introduce first. Because most animals are so motivated by treats, you might assume that "treat" or "food" would be good starter words. I certainly did, but I also quickly realized (as did a lot of us pioneers) that this was a mistake. Your learner might love this button, but the problem is that you can't feed them all the time. Not only would this button get overused, you couldn't act on the request because that would be unhealthy.

Christina Hunger's dog, Stella, began with "outside." "Outside" and "play" are great starter words that many of us using AAC recommend. In Chapter 3, we discussed consistency and modeling. "Outside" is a word that can be modeled/used multiple times per day so you, as the teacher, can press this button every time you go outside. Your learner should start to catch on that pressing a button that says "outside" precedes actually going outside.

"Outside" can be very general at first since it could entail going for a walk, going potty, or simply going outside to play. You can start to differentiate activities once your learner has caught on that these buttons mean something when they get pressed. Again, keep in mind that with that first button, your learner has a lot going on. They have to get used to the idea of pressing a button, listening to the sound, and then understanding that they get to do the thing the button just said.

If you travel with your learner or have more than one home, you might see that your learner is able to use a word like "outside" in a contextually appropriate way. This, too, is very exciting because it means they understand the concept of outside regardless of where they are.

The same goes with "play," which is another great first word. It can be modeled for both inside and outside playtime very generally. Play might mean giving your learner their favorite toy to enjoy alone. Play could also be a good game of tug of war. When outside, play might mean some fetch or frisbee time. Again, you can progress to more specific words later. For example, we now have "toy," "tug," and "frisbee" on Casper's board. This was also dictated by his favorite activities. To say that he is obsessed with his frisbee is an understatement.

Teach Your Dog to Talk

Core Words

Core words are words that will be specific to you and your family and how you communicate with your learner. In the world of AAC, core vocabulary consists of high-frequency words and makes up about 75 to 80 percent of the words we use on a daily basis. Beyond your first words, which will probably be "outside" and "play," you need to examine which words you use most with your learner. That will help you determine which words come next.

For example, do you say "potty" to mean both "pee pee" and "poo poo," or do you differentiate the two activities? Some learners are taught to use "hungry," while others have the word "food" on their board. It really depends on how you speak to your learner when referring to an activity. So, if you ask "Are you hungry?" when it's meal time, "hungry" would be a better choice. But if you say "Do you want food?" then "food" would be a more appropriate word choice.

Core words should reflect how the majority of the household speaks. Those words should be consistent when interacting with your learner.

Core words should include all members of the household—humans and animals. It's likely your learner will want to have a button to refer to someone at some point, so we have an entire HexTile just for people and animals. You can also include the words "friend" and "stranger" to differentiate between people who come to your house on an infrequent basis. This is assuming you are modeling these words to teach your dog the difference between a friend and a stranger.

As I mentioned before, teaching your dog to talk can be an insanely addictive activity, and stretching your learner's vocabulary is very rewarding as you begin to see how they put together complex thoughts using more than one or two words. Your core words may expand beyond simple wants or needs, but these are the words that will likely never come off the word board because your learner uses them as part of their everyday existence.

Fringe Words

In AAC for humans, the companion to core words are fringe words, or fringe vocabulary. These words are used with less frequency, or roughly 20 to 25 percent of the time, and are highly specific to your learner and household.

These personalized words help give your learner more communication power because it allows them to be more specific. The fringe words you use will probably change over time more than the core words. That's why it's important to reevaluate which words are on your word board to make sure you remove fringe words that aren't being used much and add ones you think your learner might be missing.

For example, one of Casper's fringe words was "golf cart," which had to be replaced once we moved and no longer owned one. Some of his other fringe words include his toys, which all have unique names, as well as places he goes and people he knows. He knows "Nonna's house" means he is going to go visit my mom (his grandmom).

Limiting Words

Another vocabulary concept to include is limiting words. There are a few options for adding words that let your learner know that something *is not* possible for whatever reason. For example, if your learner is pressing "treat" for the ten-thousandth time or asking to go "outside" and "play" at midnight, you need to be able to deny their request with a button that says some version of "no."

Casper has "all done" and "no," which we use more than he does, but it's important that they are present on the word board so we can model them. Casper will say "no" when he doesn't want to do something. Being able to create some ground rules around how the word board operates helps you maintain control instead of feeling like you're living with a tiny dictator.

We also use "later," which isn't necessarily "no" but "not right now." That button has been useful because instead of setting up a "treat" request followed by a "no" response power struggle, "later" has taught Casper that he will eventually get whatever he is asking for as long as he waits patiently. Since he understands the concept of "wait" and "later" from his obedience training, this word has been invaluable for us in responding to his demands without crushing his dreams.

There are tons of resources and books available to learn about AAC in general. Some of the concepts won't translate to your animal learner, but a lot do. I would encourage you to do more exploration into AAC if you are really interested in how language development works. It's a fascinating topic!

Adding or Subtracting Words

You may need to add or subtract words over time.

For instance, if you were to move and the "lizard" you are obsessed with (see Tai @Tai_Tai_Talks on Instagram) is no longer around, you would have to remove that button. Casper lost his beloved "golf cart" button now that we live in a neighborhood that doesn't use golf carts. Or, your learner's interests could change and they might not want to play frisbee as much as they used to.

The important thing is to constantly be aware of what words your learner is using so that the word board is an accurate reflection of their environment and interests. Again, core words probably won't change much, but fringe words might.

Recording the Words

Unless you love the sound of your own voice, give each family member a chance to record some of the words. We all recorded ourselves saying our own names so Casper could associate the names with our voices. We've had to rerecord buttons a lot because we realized that the way we were saying some words—our intonation and pitch—wasn't the way we would say the words to Casper. You do need to speak loudly and clearly when recording the word because the speaker is located on the bottom and can be muffled depending on what material you have the buzzer mounted on. The FluentPet buttons are a little better from a sound-quality standpoint, but it can still be difficult to get the word to sound like you would normally say it when you are recording it as a standalone word. Someone in my

Facebook group suggested using Siri or something similar to vocalize the word for the button recording. I don't see why this wouldn't work, but since your family is doing most of the talking in the household, I think it's best if you record the words.

Complex Words and Phrases

Once you get beyond core words, you may want to add more complex words to your learner's board. It is important to connect the word to the behavior. Model the emotion you are trying to teach by *catching* your dog feeling a certain way. For instance, if your learner is in their happy place—whether that's playing or snuggled up with you on the sofa—you could use the word "happy." On the flip side, if you notice that your learner is feeling anxious or upset, you could model the word "mad" or "sad." The point is that they need to name their feeling before they can use it on the word board.

Your dog might be "mad" if you denied them a treat or put away their favorite toy. Your learner might be "sad" if someone in the household they are particularly attached to has to leave. Find a way to delineate the differences in these emotions so you can attach them to the right word. It's definitely more challenging to do this because you have to interpret the emotions your learner might be feeling. Bunny (@whataboutbunny) has really mastered this, so I recommend checking out her Instagram feed for examples.

As you add more nuanced words, consistently evaluate whether your learner is using them in the right context. We tried teaching Casper the word "concern" since other learners—namely Bunny—had been using this word. He began using it the same way he used "help," so ultimately we decided to discontinue that word.

Again, it is important to stress that because all of this is so novel, you will be learning as you go along. Be engaged and track progress to determine which words are working for your individual learner.

Introducing Multiple Words

The Learning Resources buttons come in sets of four. A lot of people use them to start this journey. Most teachers agree that teaching word pairs like yes/no or food/water is effective because it gives your learner choices that are related to each other. These words can also be placed into the Fitzgerald Key groupings since they will likely be related to each category.

Once Casper learned his initial eight words, we ordered two more sets of buttons (eight buttons) and began filling up his board. Looking back, I don't think he really caught on to those next eight words as quickly, and it could be because we threw them at him too fast. It will depend on your learner, but I don't recommend introducing eight new buttons at once.

If you have decided to set up a way to track your learner's progress, this will help to inform you as to when to introduce a new word or word pairs.

Words Related to Time and Temperature

Many learners seem to grasp the concept of time with words such as "now" or "later" and even more advanced vocabulary like "today" or "tomorrow," or even "morning" or "night." These could be used as limiting words as well so that you aren't necessarily saying "no" but rather "not right now" when your learner makes a request. Casper often asks for things to which we have to say "<requested thing> later" back to him. For example, "Golf cart later."

Several learners I follow online know the words for temperature ("hot"/"cold") and weather. Casper hates rain and definitely understands when we tell him "no walk" or "no play" because "rain." We will then open the door to show him that it's raining and he then stops asking to go outside. Similarly, we don't go outside if it's too hot or humid. That's a little trickier because we have to stand outside for a minute before Casper realizes how hot it actually is. Usually, he will choose to come back inside on his own and immediately heads for an air conditioning vent to lie in front of.

Teaching your learner these advanced concepts isn't something everyone will want to do, but it can be useful.

Words Used to Narrate

We've focused a lot on how your learner uses vocabulary to request an action, but keep in mind, they may also use their words to narrate their own actions. When we started following Ms. Hunger, she was still relatively early in the process of exploring AAC with Stella. In one of the videos she posted on Instagram, Stella was using her word board not only to request something, but to name what she had just done. I remember thinking how cool that was, and then, about two months into his AAC training, Casper did it!

One evening, we took him out for his favorite activity, which was riding around in our golf cart. Needless to say, his "golf cart" button was overused. Anyway, we had just returned home from our evening drive, and he made a beeline for his word board and pressed "Casper" and then "golf cart." At first we were confused. We explained that we just went on a golf cart ride. About two minutes later, he pressed "all done." From that point on, he has frequently used his words to tell us about an activity that was over or "all done."

For instance, he will press, "Casper, outside, play!" and then come inside after playing and press "Casper, outside" and wander off. It took us a while to figure out that he was telling us what he had just done instead of immediately requesting to go outside again.

Missing Words

As I mentioned, I belong to several Facebook groups as well as the TheyCanTalk.org forum, and one thing that is emerging about our learners is their ability to create a word for something they need or want out of existing vocabulary.

For example, a teacher I spoke to for this book said that her learner really enjoyed playing on the trampoline with her children. As she was just getting started with AAC, she didn't have many vocabulary words on her board, but she did have the words "play" and "bed." One summer evening, her kids were outside, and her learner (a dog) was watching them from the window. He went over and pressed "play" and "bed" several times within about ten minutes. At first, she was confused, but then realized he didn't have the word for "trampoline," so he was calling it a "play bed." His bed is one of the elevated ones that sort of resembles a trampoline, so that made sense to him. She let him out and he went straight to the trampoline to jump around with the kids. Amazing!

The point in relaying this story is that you need to be open to the possibility that your learner's vocabulary will grow organically based on what their focus is. It will be important to discern what they are trying to communicate and then add the appropriate vocabulary word to their board.

Moving the Word Board

There may come a time when you either move or simply have to relocate your learner's buttons. You may also need to change words around, take a word away (if it's not being used very much), and recalibrate your setup. If this happens, go back to the beginning with modeling the button in its new location. You might also encourage your learner to simply explore the board or press buttons randomly to see what they say.

Casper did this on his own when we switched from the board to the HexTiles and when we took away some words. We didn't have the stickers for the FluentPet buttons when we first switched to using them, so I was struggling to remember where certain words were, but Casper memorized all thirty-six words perfectly in about a week.

If you are switching from one type of setup to a different one, it's best practice to do it slowly, keeping the old board close to the new setup if possible until all of the words have migrated to the new board.

If you began with buttons that were distributed throughout the house (for example, to place the word button next to the thing it references, such as the "outside" button next to the door or the "food" button near their bowls) and now want to consolidate all the words onto one board, you might try doing that slowly as well.

When we moved, we had to replace a few words to reflect our new surroundings, but because we had been narrating those activities, all we had to do was show Casper where the new words were, and he caught on quickly. The important thing is that the words reflect what is going on in your learner's environment or household. If you adopt a new animal family member or have a child, add a button to your learner's board with that family member's name.

Casper hasn't quite caught on to using Chico's name yet, but I think once he does, he'll probably let us know he's not a fan. In Casper's defense, Chico is driving him up the wall because all he wants to do is play.

Chapter 5

Tracking Progress

As I mentioned in Chapter 2, depending on the level of complexity you are planning for your learner's board, you might want to chart their progress in a formal way. This will help you determine how long it takes for your learner to use a word and if that word is indeed a useful one. We've replaced several words that just weren't working for Casper or for us.

You can also keep track of how your learner uses a word. For example, are they using a word in a novel way to communicate something else? Recall the "water" + "bone" for "ice" story or the "play" + "bed" for "trampoline" example of learners combining words to communicate something new. I'm sure you'll run across lots more examples online or even experience them for yourself. The point is that keeping track will enable you to be more aware of these novel word combinations and add words specific to your learner as necessary.

Data Tracking

Whether you use a white board, a notebook, or something more complex like a spreadsheet or Google Form, keep track of the following data points and leave some space for notes:

Date and Week

This is useful to record the buttons your learner pressed on any given day. You can also track when you introduced a button.

Word Introduction

Once you've noted the day/time you introduced a new button on your calendar, begin modeling the new word right away and note the amount of time elapsed between when the word was introduced to when your learner began using the word appropriately.

Word Use and Frequency

Note how often your learner is using a specific word, along with their most active time of day for using it. (This is where a video camera helps.) In addition to frequency, you can chart the rate of use over time to determine the utility of a word.

Again, depending on how detailed you are with tracking this data, you can begin to group your results by month to see how your learner is progressing. A simple progress sheet like the following will do. I've filled it out as an example based on how we used when we first started animal AAC with Casper.

Casper's AAC Daily Progress Sheet

Date started: 11/2/19

Today's date: 12/2/19

Week #: 4

New words: Want

Word	Number of times used
Play	II
Outside	IIII
Jerry	II
Casper	II
Want	IIII

Time of day most active (this is where the video camera footage will help): Morning

Notes:

It was a nice day outside, and Casper sat by the window a lot. He went to his word board and pressed "outside" several times, in addition to standing by the door and whining a little bit. We took him to the dog park and on a thirty-minute walk.

Video Tracking

In the beginning of the book, we discussed using video capture to keep up with your learner's progress. Having a motion-activated camera pointed at your word board is a great way to capture all the presses and be able to review the footage to make more nuanced observations.

Casper occasionally presses a button by accident, and if I'm not looking right at the board when he is doing it, I might not be able to tell that his press was a mistake. Having the video footage is a great way to see if a button didn't activate correctly or observe if your learner is more talkative during certain times of the day. It's not a requirement to have a video camera, but it does make it easier if you are interested in keeping detailed data about your learner.

Video is also great for sharing on social channels if you want to do that.

Multilearner Households

This is where it can get tricky. Depending on one learner's interest and proficiency with the buttons, it can be difficult to decide when or how to add more words without overwhelming another learner. Even in a single-learner household, introducing words too quickly can lead to frustration and "meltdowns" where the learner will start pressing all the buttons at once with no intention of communicating. This phenomenon can also be observed when a learner is hungry or tired, and it's best to redirect them to an alternate activity when this happens.

For those who have one learner who is using the buttons with regular frequency and learning at a faster clip, you can use completely separate word boards for each learner (which is what we are doing). For the learner who is a little slower, a word board with fewer words might be less intimidating.

Another option is to keep the core words that are common to each of them grouped in one section of the larger board.

Now that I have two learners, including one who is just starting out, my personal observation is that Casper will use Chico's board, but Chico doesn't dare try Casper's board yet. He's walked over to it, but seems almost intimidated by it, because he walks away from it pretty fast.

We have a four-button board for Chico by the door that has buttons for "outside," "play," "pee," "poop." Chico is just starting to show interest and has only pressed his buttons a few times. Casper, on the other hand, regularly uses Chico's board to tell us what he needs. Casper has even told us what Chico needs, which is interesting but not a unique phenomenon. Another learner named Tai (@Tai_Tai_Talks on Instagram) could sense when his new brother (who was not potty trained) needed to go out and would let their owner know by using the buttons. So, now we know that dogs can not only request something, but can also narrate their day and speak for another pet in the household.

As far as I can tell, every teacher has a slightly different approach to this, and of course, much of it depends on your space, how much room you have, and how attuned you are to which words each learner needs.

Teach Your Dog to Talk

Age of the Learner

Learners can start at all ages. Bunny began when she was a puppy, but other dogs (and cats) are just getting started at age five or beyond. Casper was about a year and a half when he started.

No matter your learner's age, you will still follow their progression based on their understanding of how to use the buttons and their meaning. Speak the words you have decided to use consistently—especially the core words, which are the most important—at first. Have an agreed-upon vocabulary list you and other members of your household will use with your learner.

The rate of learning will obviously depend on the species and breed. As more data is gathered, we may have a better answer as to optimum timing to begin working with your learner, but even the little bit of data we have right now shows that you can indeed "teach an old dog new tricks."

Animal AAC and Beyond

Chico has just begun obedience training. Even though his trainer doesn't know much about AAC for dogs, she thinks some basic obedience training before starting can help with focus and prevent unwanted behaviors such as destroying the buttons. Again, it will depend on your learner, but a calm, focused dog is going to be able to learn this new skill more quickly.

Chico's trainer is very intrigued by the possibilities presented by combining AAC with behavioral training, but she said it's best to address problematic behaviors before starting something that requires more focus, like learning AAC.

We also discussed the implications of AAC for service animals. Imagine a service animal being able to "talk" to a first responder, for instance. They might be able to "tell" them what happened to their owner or some other important information. It sounds far-fetched when I write that, but here's why I think it could eventually happen.

Teach Your Dog to Talk

Casper only communicates with us, but recently we had our HVAC worked on, so we were in a different area of the house for a lot of the time the technicians were over. Apparently Casper needed to go outside and was able to get one of the service technician's attention. He went to his board and pressed "Casper," "pee pee." The technician then came down to the basement to let us know our dog needed a potty break. Also, they could not stop laughing at the fact that our dog just told them he needed to go pee.

That was the first time we had seen Casper use his word board to communicate with someone other than our family. Since then, he uses it pretty regularly with visitors. Our dog sitter has a video on her Instagram of Casper requesting "scritches" from her.

Levels

Not to be repetitive, but this field of study (which really encompasses several fields of study, including but not limited to cognitive science, animal behavior, and animal training) is an ever-changing one, so what is written today might be outdated in a year. That being said, the TheyCanTalk.org forum came up with this system to help you identify where your learner is in terms of their progress. I added Level 5 because I feel like some learners are already outstripping what is considered the highest level.

Level 0

Your learner is being introduced to this foreign concept of buttons that say words. They may be confused. It works well to place the first button near whatever it is referencing. If you begin with "outside," that button would be near the door, for example. In this stage, you are the button pusher. This is the beginning of modeling behavior, which will guide your learner through the next levels. This is also the stage when you will need the most patience. It could be weeks before you hear or observe your learner's first button press.

Level 1

Your learner has leveled up once they know how to press a button with their snout or paw. The key here is for you to respond and do whatever the button says. Again, if "outside" is the first button, take your learner outside. They will eventually connect that a button press that says "outside" means they get to go outside.

Level 2

Your learner has reached this level if they have two or more words that you are modeling for them, and they are interested in this activity. They still may not fully grasp the meaning of each word or how it is tied to an action, but if they are curious, this is a good sign.

Level 3

This level is exciting because you see that your learner has made the connection between the button and the thing it says. They are using the button consistently and appropriately. They may also be looking to you for a reaction. Begin planning for your next word or words.

Level 4

Your learner is using multiple buttons, whether they are distributed in various locations or consolidated onto a word board. For most teachers/learners, this would be anywhere from four to twelve words, enough for a learner to communicate their basic wants and needs without taking up too much space in your home.

Level 5

The advanced learners have reached this level when they not only use multiple buttons, but have also begun to understand abstract concepts, time and place references, and can even answer questions when given choices or respond "yes" or "no."

Remember Why You Started

Being a part of this community is really exciting. We help and support each other regularly in the various Facebook groups, via direct messages, and on the TheyCanTalk.org forum.

However, in the age of likes, comments, and followers (which can even mean real money and merchandise) on social media, it could be easy to get carried away. As long as both you and your learner are having fun, this should be a beneficial activity for all involved. If, however, you notice that using the buttons is becoming stressful for your learner or you, take a step back and figure out why. Don't push your learner to use new buttons just for the sake of expanding their vocabulary so you can show them off on social media. Let this process evolve organically. Be patient. I know I keep saying that, but it's really important that this activity remain a positive experience for both you and your learner.

Casper has reached a plateau of thirty-six words. Even those get swapped out with some degree of regularity based on usage or inactivity. I think any more than that could overwhelm him and, perhaps, us. The point is, each learner is unique, and their progress is what it is. I didn't set out to have my dog go viral, and while it's been fun, I think most of us would continue this activity even in the absence of social media. Heck, we're not doing much posting right now because I'm writing this book! (I promise to get back to making fun dog videos once this is done!)

That being said, as long as you can stay objective about why you are ultimately doing this—in other words, NOT for likes, comments, and followers—then there is nothing wrong with posting videos of your learner and sharing their gifts with the world. It's been so incredible to follow along and watch so many animals communicating with their owners.

Below is a small sample of learners who are pretty active on social media. Once I'm done writing this book, I'll be back on TikTok (@casper_borderaussie) and Instagram (@casper_borderaussie). In the meantime, learners on this list are worth watching to learn tips and tricks and also because they are very entertaining. I couldn't include every account I love, so make sure to search some of the popular hashtags like #theycantalk or #animalaac to find some amazing talking animals.

Dogs

@bastianandbrews on IG and TikTok

@whataboutbunny on IG and TikTok

@thechattylab on IG and TikTok

@Tai_Tai_Talks on IG and TikTok

@HoneyButterTalks on IG and TikTok

@flambothedog on IG and TikTok

@picklesandpeachspeak on IG and TikTok

@wafflestheyorkie_ on IG and @wafflestheyorkie TikTok

@oski_the_pug on IG and TikTok

@barnum_the_talking_dog on IG and TikTok

Cats

@billispeaks on IG and TikTok

@catmanjohn on IG and TikTok

@thedailysteveb on IG

Horse

Lira the Horse @liralearns on IG or @shehorse on TikTok

Reptile

@lizardinglessons on IG

Birds

Peahens Artemis and Eris use the buttons on the Kadreeva Whitemane YouTube channel.

Chapter 6

Keep Talking!

Are y'all having fun yet?

It cannot be overstated that the main goal of exploring AAC with your learner is not only to deepen your connection with them, but also to have fun and enjoy learning about their personality. *Are* we crazy dog people? Of course! But we're also crazy *about* our dogs (or cats/lizards/lemurs/pigs/peacocks) and this is a fun activity with real benefits. As mentioned, people report that their learners have fewer behavioral challenges once they begin using AAC. You should be very proud of this progress yourself and enjoy this new form of interspecies communication!

I've learned that Casper likes my husband more. If you've seen some of our videos on TikTok or YouTube, you'll understand what I'm talking about. Casper will press combinations of "Jerry," "where," "go," and "look" whenever Jerry is away or is just in another room. The only time he's not a fan of my husband is if Jerry has to discipline him. He will then walk over to his board and press "Jerry," "go" immediately afterward. This has happened a handful of times, and each time it's funny because Casper obviously does not like being told what to do. I'm sure if he could open the door and point, he would be gesturing for Jerry to leave the house—"Jerry. Go!" All dogs' personalities are unique, obviously, and it's interesting that giving them this communication skill really enhances your understanding of who they are.

Casper also doesn't like it when people don't keep their word. In one interaction that went very viral on TikTok, Casper got mad at my daughter because she promised to take him on a golf cart ride but couldn't because it started raining. Casper, of course, didn't know why his planned golf cart ride wasn't happening, but he felt it necessary to let me know that he was mad that Eleanor had broken her promise to him. It was remarkable to see him processing his frustration and being able to communicate with me that he wasn't getting to go for a ride in his beloved golf cart. It was also hilarious. Moments like these are happening all the time with so many AAC learners that it's hard to keep up. I spend way too much time on TikTok, Instagram, and YouTube watching videos of all these amazing animals.

Capturing our learners' interactions with us or their surroundings is a joy. Being able to share these videos on social media brings everyone along for the ride. Whether it's a heartwarming interaction like Casper pressing "love you" for the first time or something funny like Bastian (@bastianandbrews) and his overly enthusiastic button presses requesting a "treat," the idea of a "talking dog" or any other animal is still a novel concept and entertaining to watch.

I recently came across an account on TikTok for Waffles the Yorkie (@wafflestheyorkie). At the time of this writing, he has nearly 1.1 million followers and 11.1 million likes. Yes, he's adorable because, duh, Yorkie. *But get this*: his owner/teacher has also built a word board for him to use swear words. When we first started, my husband joked that it would be funny to add a swear word or two to Casper's word board. I figured someone might eventually do it, and Waffles doesn't disappoint. While it might be offensive to some people, I think his videos are hilarious. If he doesn't get a treat, he presses his "a**hole" button. He has quite the "potty mouth," as his owner says.

Does he really understand the meaning behind these words? Who knows? The point is that this is an example of a teacher having fun with this activity. Waffles even has a swear jar (!) and has gotten his buttons taken away from him because he was swearing too much.

I'm sure that as this activity grows in size and scope, we will see more funny examples of owners and their learners communicating in inventive ways.

According to *Today's Veterinary Business*, an estimated 11.38 million US households have gotten a new pet during the pandemic.[5] If even a portion of those new owners decide to explore AAC with their learners, we will see an explosion of animals learning to communicate.

---

5 "Pets Remain in High Demand during COVID," *Today's Veterinary Business*, October 2020, https://todaysveterinarybusiness.com/pets-appa -survey-covid.

POV: Your Dog

Ever since I began this activity with Casper, I've wondered what he thinks of his newfound skills. Perhaps he doesn't even view them as new skills since he's obviously understood much of what we've been saying *to* him since he was a puppy. I would think he's happy to have some tools to talk back to us rather than just listening and following commands.

In her latest children's novel, *The One and Only Bob*, author Katherine Applegate wrote about dogs and language, but from the dog Bob's point of view. It's kind of how you'd imagine a dog would write a book or tell a story:

Bob says he's never met a dog who didn't perk up when hearing the word "walk" and tells the reader that dogs definitely understand more than we think. He goes on to debunk the theory that dogs are only as smart as the average toddler—he estimates by about a "million" times.

When he saw Chaser on a television show, he wondered why the narrator was so impressed by the fact that Chaser knew over a thousand words because, duh, of course they understand words—some dogs more than others. He says it really depends on how interesting their owner is and if they are using fun words like "treat," "walk," "frisbee," or "bacon." Dogs also hear what he calls "swear" words, which include "vet," "bath," "fireworks," and "vacuum cleaner."

It's a cute book and a great reminder that dogs *understanding* language isn't a new phenomenon. Dogs using language is.

My childhood dog understood the word "bath," even when we spelled it out. If anyone in the house said, "The dog needs a B-A-T-H," he would disappear immediately, and it would sometimes take us a while to find him.

In my household, we've always come up with a voice for our dogs, which is a collective imagining of how we think he or she would sound if they could talk. I can't imagine we are the only people who do this?

Our last dog, a golden retriever named Nacho, had a sort of nervous and tentative voice in our minds.

That was his personality, too—suspicious and scared of everything, from water to grocery bags to all the typical stuff like fireworks and thunder.

For some inexplicable reason other than the fact that we live in Georgia, Casper started out with a genteel southern drawl, so that was how we would "speak" on his behalf. After he learned to use his buttons, though, we slowly shifted his voice to a mid-Atlantic, almost British accent. It was subconscious, but made sense when I began thinking about it. We now viewed Casper as being a bit more formal since he could use words, so our voice for him changed to reflect that.

When the company Crown & Paw approached us to help advertise their pet portraits (where they put your pet's head onto the body of a human) in exchange for a free painting, it was only natural that we chose the British admiral for Casper. Needless to say, this portrait hangs in our living room next to some other prized pieces of art.

From Family Pet to Content Creator

Were it not for social media—specifically TikTok—I would not be writing this book. I mean, I might have *thought* about writing this book, but I was too busy making fun videos with my dog. I didn't have much else to do at the time because we were in the midst of the pandemic. Even though I had begun working on this project in pre-COVID-19 times, it really got underway when we didn't have much else to do.

I opened a TikTok account for my dog so I could keep tabs on my kids without having to sign up for my own account. I had a few cute videos of Casper, but didn't expect to really do anything with this app other than post a few videos every so often while I was scoping out what my kids were up to online.

Within about a week of signing up and posting our first video of Casper pressing the "love you" button, it had been viewed millions of times and our account had gained over 50,000 followers. My daughter was so jealous!

There were a few other really impressive "talking dogs" we were friends with on other social media platforms so, of course, we told them to sign up for TikTok as well. One of those smart doggos, Bunny (@whatabout bunny), now has 6.7 million followers and is a superstar both on social media and the world of AAC. Her vocabulary is very impressive and her owner, Alexis, is extremely dedicated to this endeavor. I love watching Bunny's complex thought processes.

Anyway, we turned making TikTok videos into a fun family activity, and it was a great distraction from what was going on in the world at the time.

The *Wall Street Journal* did a great article featuring some of the early breakout stars who came after Stella.[6] Bunny the Sheepadoodle (@whataboutbunny), Casper (@casper_borderaussie), Billi the Cat (@billispeaks), Beans the Dog, Silke the dog (@koning.silke) and her guinea pig pals, and another cat named Bix. Of course, there was much skepticism around many of these early reports of animals learning to communicate using words, but for the most part, people appreciated seeing our adorable and often hilarious learners.

It's genuinely heartwarming to know that you've brightened someone's day with your cute animal videos, and while we aren't as active as we were when we were all at home together, I'm hoping once I'm finished writing this, I can get back to posting videos of Casper—and now Chico, as he navigates his expanding word board.

---

6 James Cordilia, "Tired of the People in Your Family? Some Are Teaching Their Dogs to Talk," *The Wall Street Journal*, August 14, 2020.

I've also made some really nice online friends whom I hope to meet in person one day. I'm a giant fan of many of the other learners on social media, and I love seeing their progress. It's hugely entertaining.

As long as you enjoy being a content creator, talking dogs are the new cat videos of the internet. People can't seem to get enough of them. Except the fun-ruiners...

Fun-Ruiners

This isn't a word but should be because they exist and will always be out there. Fun-ruiners, who simply reject outright that any of what they are seeing is true and leave no room for being persuaded otherwise, are everywhere.

Whether you decide to go the route of posting videos publicly on social media or sharing your learner's progress with just friends and family, you will inevitably encounter the person who says some version of the following: "Your dog is just pressing random buttons, and you're adding your own interpretation to these random presses." *Ugh*.

Because this is all so new, it's easy to let comments like this take the wind out of your sails. After all, you introduced a button, and your learner used it in a contextually appropriate way! You then fulfilled their request, and your learner is now content. *You* know they are learning to communicate using AAC, so that's all that matters. Sure, you could get into how if animals didn't understand language, they couldn't follow basic obedience commands, but debating the finer points of animal linguistics isn't why people post negative comments.

As with most fun-ruiners, it's best to ignore them. Fortunately, most of the feedback we and others get is supportive. This community of learners is growing every day, and we all naturally support each other. You can always delete and block out the negative comments, but don't let them get you down if you are enjoying exploring AAC with your learner.

Don't Give Up!

As with any hobby, sometimes your interest in it waxes and wanes. That's okay. If you have reached a plateau with your learner either because you feel like they don't actually need more words or you've run out of space to add new words, it might start to feel less exciting.

Since we've been at this for over a year and a half, we've certainly gone through periods when we all use the word board less. We don't model words as much, and that keeps Casper from using it as much, too. That's okay. We've found it's easy to pick back up where we left off. Moving definitely put a dent in our ability to be as consistent with Casper as we would have wanted to be. But, now that we have another learner in the house, we're all eager to teach him AAC and have been more consistent with modeling.

Hopefully you, as an AAC enthusiast, will use this with your learner for their lifetime and with any future animals you add to your family. Remember that half the responsibility of picking up this skill falls to you as the teacher. You worked hard to learn how to model using the buttons, choose the right words for your learner, be consistent, and build a functional word board.

One way to keep this hobby fresh is to constantly reassess the utility of the words on the board. Even though you may only have room for a certain number of words, you can always take away those that aren't being used very much or are obsolete for whatever reason. That will give you an opportunity to introduce and model a fun new word. Seeing your learner make the connection between a new button or word and a new thing or activity never gets old. When Casper lost "golf cart" because we moved, he had to learn "backyard" since we now had one. Guess who *loves* the backyard? Now if we could just interest him in the swimming pool.

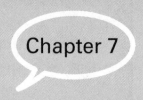

Chapter 7

Resources

The number of websites, articles, videos, and online tools seems to be growing by the day, which is awesome! As of this writing, here are a few great places to start your AAC journey.

Books and Websites

HungerForWords.com. Christina Hunger's website *Hunger For Words* is an excellent resource for anyone who wants to learn more from her perspective as a speech-language pathologist. Before she published her book, she had a great blog (which is now just a website), where so many of us went for up-to-the-minute information. It continues to be the top resource for all beginning learners, even those of us who have been at it for a while. Her book is great, and her website and subscription newsletter contain lots of additional information. Check out each section of the website, from the FAQs to recommended products. Stella's journey is a remarkable story, and the website includes more recommended reading about AAC.

TalktotheBeans.com. This website is run by a cat behaviorist who has a talking cat.

AAC-Specific Online Groups and Forums

There is no one-size-fits-all approach to animal AAC. There are only best practices, and they will evolve over time. Having a good sounding board of individuals who may have encountered the same roadblocks is really motivating and keeps you on track.

Your learner may hit a plateau, lose interest, or take a break from using certain buttons. You'll find someone in these online groups who has been through that before and perhaps get some good feedback to help you and your learner push past those obstacles.

I have been a part of several online groups since I began using AAC with Casper. The Facebook groups are useful for asking general questions, especially when you are first starting out.

Hunger for Words Fan Experiments

This Facebook group started shortly after Christina Hunger went public with her Instagram videos and blog. We're all huge Stella fans, obviously, and love supporting one another as we learn alongside each other. The group has over four thousand members and is pretty active.

https://www.facebook.com/groups/548114165978352

Exploring Canine & Feline AAC

This Facebook group has about three thousand members and, as the name specifies, includes cats. Members are generally very helpful and supportive.

https://www.facebook.com/groups/414909282513039

They Can Talk

Created by the founders of CleverPet and FluentPet, this community-generated site inspired by the work of Christina Hunger is dedicated to helping learners communicate using AAC devices. The site and associated forum bring together tips and tricks, do's and don'ts, as well as comments and feedback on a wide range of topics from a great network of supportive people who are constantly discovering new things and overcoming problems about teaching words to dogs. Each day covers a new topic, such as Milestone Mondays and That's Interesting Thursdays.

https://how.theycantalk.org/c/home

Enrichment Resources

In the process of delving into the world of AAC, my family and I have also turned our attention to various types of enrichment activities for Casper and Chico. Canine enrichment (and by extension, other species-specific enrichment) is a natural extension of what you are doing by engaging your dog beyond what most owners have typically done with their pets.

A dog's brain needs stimulation in the form of their innate behaviors. Casper is a super chewer so he gets a lot of opportunities to chew on various toys and textures. He also enjoys chasing things, scent work, and scavenging. In addition to his word board, he has a lot of contraptions that we've either built or bought to feed these behaviors and keep him happy from both a physical and emotional standpoint.

AAC is a type of enrichment activity, but it isn't an innate behavior, so it's important to balance out their AAC work with a lot of playing, sniffing, and scavenging. Ms. Hunger touches on this in Chapter 10 of her book, when discussing Maslow's Hierarchy of Needs, a theory developed by Abraham Maslow to explain that humans cannot move on to higher pursuits without having their foundational needs met. When you extrapolate that concept to your dog, this means that your learner will be able to perform at their highest level of potential as long as their basic needs are met in the form of food, shelter, rest, safety, and security. So, if they are tired and hungry, they aren't going to be able to focus properly on learning a new word or understanding AAC in general.

There is a Facebook group called Canine Enrichment Ideas (https://www.facebook.com/groups/23264240 80971527), which has a lot of good posts related to enrichment activities.

I realize this is a book about teaching your dog to talk, but a happy, well-adjusted, calm dog/animal is more likely to be receptive to learning to communicate using AAC. I recommend exploring the following tools with your learner.

- 🐾 LickiMats. These are textured mats that you spread something like yogurt or peanut butter on (freezing it is a great idea because it extends the time it takes for your dog to lick the mat clean).

- 🐾 Snuffle Mat. This can be either made or purchased and is great for letting your dog forage for food and keeping them from eating too fast. It's usually made from felt or fabric. You can also just twirl up some old fabric and place their kibble inside to let them work to find it. We also put treats or kibble inside cardboard boxes.

- 🐾 Brain Games and Puzzles. These can get progressively harder as your dog learns to use them. We just ordered a PupPod (puppod.com)—a game with a treat dispenser connected to a pod or rocker, which dogs press when they hear it beep—for Casper. As he gets more proficient, the device, which is connected to your phone via an app, gets more difficult.

What I like about the PupPod is that it encourages the dog to use their paw to interact with the rocker portion of the toy, which is separate from the unit that spits out the treats. If your learner is struggling with learning to press buttons, this would be a great introductory toy to get them used to that particular action. The only downside is the cost ($299), but so far, I've been really impressed with it. Casper is on Level 3, and Chico is on Level 2.

🐾 Plastic Kiddie Pool. Fill this with balls, with treats hidden underneath them. This is one of Chico's favorite ways to get treats, and it keeps him engaged for a while.

General Training

As I mentioned in the first part of this book, training is important for your learner. While not everyone can afford professional training, it's important for your dog to understand basic obedience concepts and be able to respond to those cues. There are quite a few online trainers. Due to the pandemic, many experts began offering training via Zoom or videos. However, lots of videos are available for free on YouTube, Instagram, and TikTok.

Acknowledgments

To my wonderful dynamic duo at Ulysses Press: Thank you, Claire Sielaff, who believed in me as a first-time author. Your words of encouragement led me to one of the most challenging and rewarding projects I have ever undertaken. I got to write a book about something I love doing, and I'm very grateful you reached out to me. To Renee Rutledge, my amazing project manager and editor, who helped keep me on track and provided amazing feedback during those times when I got a little stuck. You make it look so easy! Thank you for everything!

To Christina Hunger, for figuring out that dogs (and other animals!) have a "voice," and encouraging us all to try these amazing tools with our own furry friends.

Training my dogs in AAC has been an incredible journey and a lifelong hobby I will replicate with all future pets. You and Stella are our heroes!

To my children, Eleanor and Blair, for giving me the time and space to write this book on weekends and late at night. Your encouragement meant everything and helped me to keep going even when I had a terrible case of writer's block.

To my husband, Jerry. You've supported every creative endeavor I have ever tried. I love you for that! Thank you for the late-night snack trays and glasses of wine you brought me to help keep me going.

And, finally, to all the animal parents out there working hard to learn this amazing new skill with your learner. I hope this book will be a good resource for you and that you and your learner will be able to use what I have written to develop a deeper relationship through communication.

About the Author

Stephanie Rocha, talking-animal aficionado and accidental TikTok creator, wants to live in a world where everyone is the person their dog (or cat) thinks they are.

With a diverse career spanning politics, business, and many creative endeavors, she's finally putting that English degree to work along with the help of her trusty sidekick—her talking Border Aussie named Casper, who is currently negotiating his ghostwriting contract.

When she's not conversing with her dog, she enjoys being a portrait photographer, binge-watching Netflix shows, and learning new dance moves to embarrass her two children on social media.